DIESEL LOCOMOTIVES

TRAINS

Lynn M. Stone

The Rourke Corporation, Inc.
Vero Beach, Florida 32964

PHOTO CREDITS:
Cover, p. 4, 10, 12, 21 © Lynn M. Stone; title page, p. 8, 13 © George H Drury; p. 7 courtesy of Union Pacific Railroad Museum Collection; p. 15, 18 from East West Rail Scenes; p. 17 © Don Hennen.

PRODUCED BY:
East Coast Studios, Merritt Island, Florida

EDITORIAL SERVICES:
Penworthy Learning Systems

Library of Congress Cataloging-in-Publication Data

Stone, Lynn M.
    Diesel locomotives / by Lynn M. Stone
        p. cm. — (Trains)
    Summary: Describes the history and uses of diesel locomotives, the different types, and some famous models.
    ISBN 0-86593-521-1
    1. Diesel locomotives Juvenile literature. [1. Locomotives. 2. Railroads—Trains.] I. Title. II. Series: Stone, Lynn M. Trains.
TJ605.5.S75 1999
625.26'6—dc21   99-13279
                                                                             CIP

Printed in the USA

TABLE OF CONTENTS

DIESEL LOCOMOTIVES

Nearly all the North American train **locomotives** (LO kuh MO tivz) in use today are diesel, or diesel-electrics.

Diesel locomotives burn diesel fuel, which is a kind of oil. Some cars and trucks also burn diesel fuel.

Diesel locomotives began to replace steam locomotives in North America in the 1930s. North American railroads now own more than 20,000 diesel-electric locomotives.

Modern diesel locomotives haul nearly all the trains in North America.

EARLY DIESEL LOCOMOTIVES

In the 1890s, a German named Rudolf Diesel invented the engine that bears his name. By 1925, a small diesel locomotive had been put into use. But the first diesel in regular rail service in North America was the Chicago, Burlington and Quincy Railroad's *Zephyr* in 1934.

The *Zephyr* looked very different from steam locomotives. It was a sleek, streamlined locomotive with a "nose" almost shovel shaped.

In the 1930s the Union Pacific Railroad's City of Los Angeles was pulled by a streamlined General Motors diesel, one of the first built.

RISE OF DIESEL POWER

Diesel engines that followed the *Zephyr* in the 1930s and 1940s had a new look. They were streamlined, too, and most of them were brightly painted. But railroads were not buying only "looks." The diesels simply ran better and more cheaply than steam locomotives.

Diesels could travel at higher average speeds. They didn't need nearly as many repairs when they were in use. And they could travel longer without stops for fuel and water. The railroad companies soon knew that diesel locomotives were in their future.

General Motors' bulldog-nosed "F" diesels were the most popular long-haul diesels of the 1940s and early 1950s.

By the end of World War II (1941-1945), more than 3,000 diesel locomotives were on American rails. During the next 10 years, diesels quickly replaced steam locomotives. In 1955, American railroads had nearly 25,000 diesel locomotives and fewer than 6,000 steam. By 1960, diesels had almost completely taken over the rails from steam.

By 1955, more than 70 American railroads owned GM's streamlined "E" and "F" series diesels.

An old rear-cab diesel switcher hauls tank cars at a freight yard.

General purpose diesels, like this General Motors GP7, or "Geep," became popular in the 1950s.

TYPES OF DIESEL LOCOMOTIVES

Diesel locomotives have been built in many shapes and sizes for many different uses. For example, the **cab** (KAB) has been placed at the front, rear, and in the middle of different diesel locomotives.

The cab is the engineer's space. Diesel locomotives without a cab are called "B" units, boosters, or slaves. They give extra power to the main locomotive, or "A" unit. An A-B-A group of locomotives would have two main locomotives with a booster unit between them.

Santa Fe's San Diegan *is led out of Los Angeles by an "A" unit diesel and its "B" unit booster in 1971.*

Most diesels are built for "yard" or "road" work. A railroad yard is where many train cars are moved around. Train cars there are **coupled** (KUP uld) together in "new" trains or taken apart as trains enter the yard.

Yard diesels are smaller, less powerful than road diesels. Yard diesels, or **switchers** (SWICH erz), switch cars from one track to another.

Road locomotives haul trains long distances on the open rails, or "road." A road locomotive may be built for freight or hauling passengers. General purpose diesels have been made for a variety of jobs.

The center-cab design was a popular type of yard switcher.

FAMOUS DIESELS

General Motors built a bulb-nosed diesel in the late 1930s for the Union Pacific Railroad. Like other early diesels, it was soon replaced by the stylish "E" unit and the famous "F," built from 1939-1960.

Meanwhile, the American Locomotive Company (Alco) built its famous PA diesels from 1946-1953. PA's in the Santa Fe Railroad's "war bonnet" design may have been the most handsome diesel locomotives ever built.

In 1968, an aging set of Santa Fe Alco PA's rested on the tracks in Bakersfield, California.

DIESEL POWER AT WORK

Diesel-electric locomotives are power plants on wheels. The diesel oil-burning engine in a locomotive runs a **generator** (JEN uh RAY tur). A generator makes electricity. Electricity sent to the locomotive's wheels moves the train.

The newest diesel engines are more powerful than earlier models. The most powerful of the old "F" diesels had 1,750 **horsepower** (HAWRS POW er). One locomotive can haul what used to take two. Some of the big locomotives have 6,500 horsepower. New locomotives will have even more horsepower.

Modern "A" units roar around a turn on the Burlington Northern Santa Fe rails at Rochelle, Illinois.

The big engines are used to pull freight trains of up to 200 cars. The longest freight trains still need several locomotives. Sometimes six or eight are coupled together.

Not all new diesel-electrics are giants. Smaller locomotives work as yard switchers and as passenger locomotives.

GLOSSARY

cab (KAB) — a part of a locomotive where the engineer and others ride to operate the controls and view the tracks

coupled (KUP uld) — attached or linked together by railroad car couplers

generator (JEN uh RAY tur) — machine in which fuel can be burned to make electric power

horsepower (HAWRS POW er) — a unit to measure an engine's ability to produce force

locomotive (LO kuh MO tiv) — a power plant or engine on wheels used to push or pull railroad cars; a train engine

switcher (SWICH er) — a locomotive made to move trains in railroad yards

INDEX

FURTHER READING

Find out more about trains with these helpful books and information sites:
Riley, C.J. *The Encyclopedia of Trains and Locomotives*. Metro Books, 1995

Association of American Railroads online at www.aar.org
California State Railroad Museum online at www.csrmf.org
Union Pacific Railroad online at http://www.uprr.com